You Can Draw

SPACE

Jordan McGill

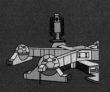

AV2

www.av2books.com

Step 1
Go to **www.av2books.com**

Step 2
Enter this unique code

FGJZAL4PB

Step 3
Explore your interactive eBook!

AV2 is optimized for use on any device

Your interactive eBook comes with...

Contents
Browse a live contents page to easily navigate through resources

Audio
Listen to sections of the book read aloud

Videos
Watch informative video clips

Weblinks
Gain additional information for research

Try This!
Complete activities and hands-on experiments

Key Words
Study vocabulary, and complete a matching word activity

Quizzes
Test your knowledge

Slideshows
View images and captions

... and much, much more!

2

You Can Draw

SPACE

CONTENTS

EXPLORING SPACE

Outer space, often simply called space, is made up of almost empty regions of the universe beyond Earth. Human trips into space have taught people a great deal about space. However, the farthest humans have traveled is to the Moon.

Some spacecrafts without pilots have traveled beyond our solar system. By learning more about the universe, we also learn more about ourselves and our own planet.

WHY DRAW?

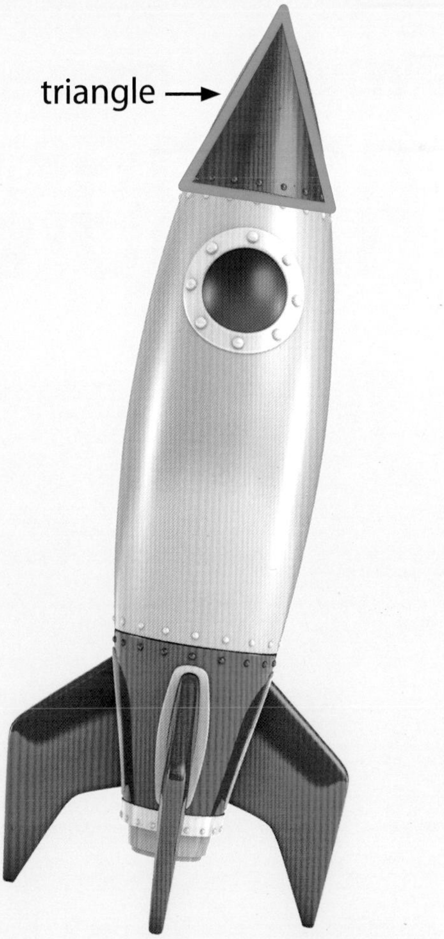

triangle ⟶

Drawing objects from space and the technologies people have invented to study space is a great way to learn. You can learn about how the objects interact and what they do.

Look around you. The world is made of shapes and lines. By combining simple shapes and lines, anything can be drawn. A planet is just a circle with a few details added. The top of a rocket can be a triangle. Almost anything, no matter how complicated, can be broken down into simple shapes.

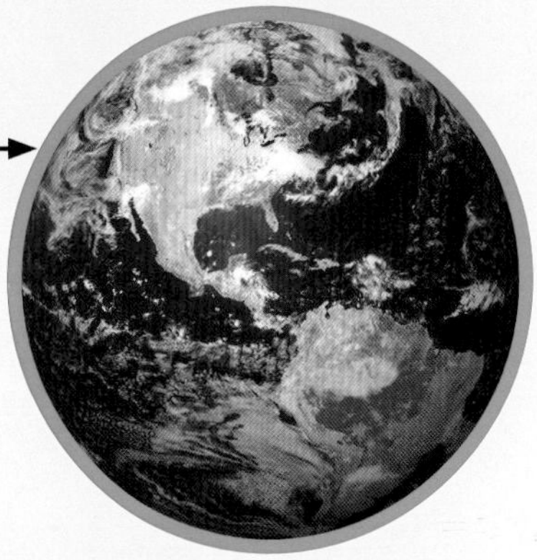

circle ⟶

What shapes do you see in this satellite?

What Is an
ASTRONAUT?

Astronauts are people trained to travel in a spacecraft and work in space. Astronauts cannot leave their spacecraft without spacesuits. These protective suits allow astronauts to stay in space for up to eight hours.

A spacesuit is a key piece of equipment for anyone heading into space. Astronauts wear these suits when they are lifting off from Earth, during landing, and anytime they are outside of their spacecraft in space. The suit provides protection when astronauts encounter the harsh environment found in space.

Helmet
The helmet keeps pressure at the right level to allow the astronaut to breathe. The front bubble is coated in a thin layer of gold to filter the Sun's harmful rays.

Control Panel
Using the control panel, an astronaut can control the **life support** systems of the suit.

Gloves
Spacesuit gloves are made of two main layers. The internal layer is like a rubber balloon surrounded by cloth, which keeps the gloves' shape. The outer layer protects the astronaut from **space debris** and extreme temperatures.

Life Support Systems

Worn like a backpack, the primary life support subsystem, or PLSS, provides astronauts with oxygen. It also filters out carbon dioxide, provides the astronaut with drinking water, and controls temperature.

White Top-Layer

Spacesuits are white because white reflects heat. This keeps astronauts cool. Temperatures under direct sunlight can reach more than 275° Fahrenheit (135° Celsius).

How to Draw an
ASTRONAUT

1) Start with a stick figure frame of the astronaut. Draw a circle for the head, ovals for the hands and feet, and lines for the body and limbs.

2) Now, draw the shape of the helmet and torso.

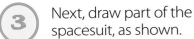

3 Next, draw part of the spacesuit, as shown.

4 Complete the spacesuit and draw the shoes.

5 In this step, add the jacket sleeves and draw the hands.

6 Draw the helmet screen and the backpack.

7 Now, add details to the spacesuit and the backpack, as shown.

8 Erase the extra lines and the stick figure.

9 Color the picture.

What Are MOON BASES?

Scientists have begun to make plans for a lunar research station, or Moon base. Scientists could stay there for months, collecting data and performing experiments. The Moon base would need housing, laboratories, and lunar vehicles. Everything would be designed to support humans in a place where there is very little air and the temperatures are extreme.

1972
The last year humans set foot on the Moon.

238,855
The average distance from Earth to the Moon, in miles. (384,400 kilometers)

Expandable Design
A Moon base should grow over time. Most Moon base designs allow for additional structures to be added.

Habitation
A Moon base would need a place for scientists to live. It would contain sleeping quarters, showers, and a kitchen.

Communication
Astronauts need to **communicate** with Earth while they are on the Moon. A communication system would allow them to maintain contact with Earth.

Power Storage
One part of the station would contain power storage units. They collect energy from the Sun and store it for use in the base. This provides energy for life support systems inside the base.

Surface Vehicle
A Moon base would need some form of transportation for scientists to travel on the Moon.

How to Draw a
MOON BASE

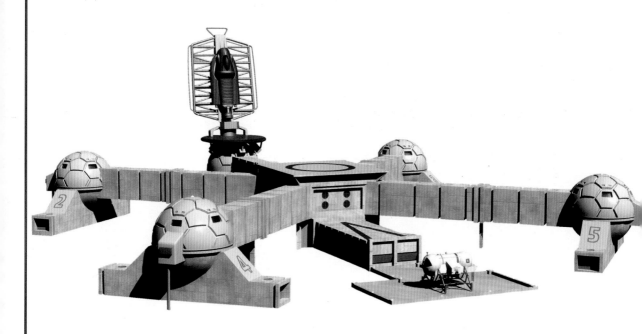

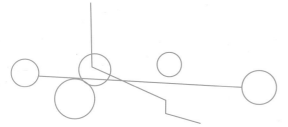

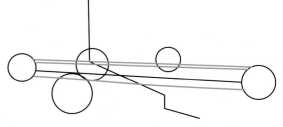

1. Start by drawing a stick figure frame of the Moon base. Use circles for the spheres and lines for the body.

2. Now, draw three parallel lines across the figure, as shown.

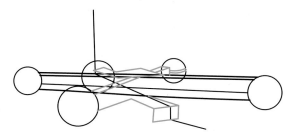

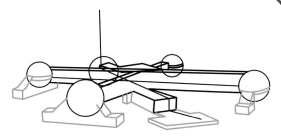

3 Next, draw the central part of the Moon base, as shown.

4 Draw the platforms, as shown.

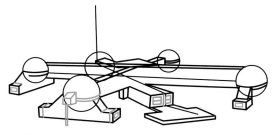

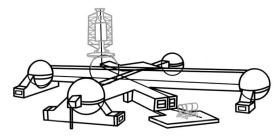

5 In this step, draw the remaining pieces, as shown.

6 Draw the antenna and a vehicle on the figure frame.

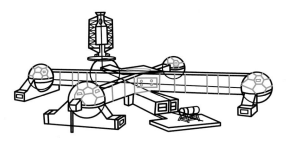

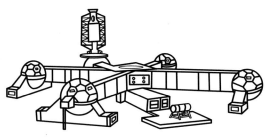

7 Now, add details to the spheres and central part, as shown.

8 Erase the extra lines and the stick figure.

9 Color the picture.

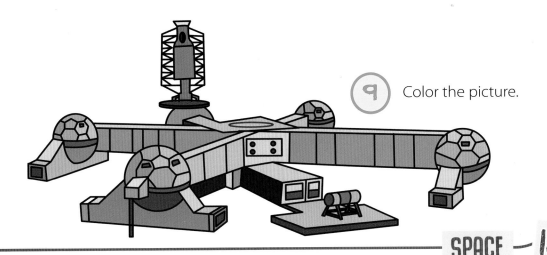

What Are
ROVERS?

The first rover to land on Mars was Sojourner in 1997. Sojourner's ability to move over the planet's surface allowed scientists to explore new places. Since then, three other rovers have landed successfully on Mars. The rovers gather information from different parts of the planet. This increases scientists' understanding of the planet's geology and the materials that form its surface. **NASA** plans to send another rover to Mars in 2020.

Antennae
The antennae allow scientists on Earth to send and receive information through a **radio system**.

Suspension
The wheels are connected to a suspension system that ensures the rover can move across rough terrain. The wheels can move up and down to cross gaps and rocky areas.

0.015
The speed Sojourner traveled in miles per hour. (0.024 km per hour)

550+
The number of photos of Mars that Sojourner sent back to Earth.

Cameras

Rovers have cameras for two purposes. Some cameras are used to navigate. The other cameras are used to collect images of Mars' surface.

Solar Panels

Today's rovers are mostly powered by solar panels. Solar panels collect energy from the Sun's rays and store it.

Wheels

Today's rovers have six wheels. Each wheel has tiny **cleats** that grip the rocky surface.

Instruments

Mars rovers have different instruments they use to collect data. Some tools include magnets to pick up and test minerals and grinders to break and collect rock samples.

How to Draw a
ROVER

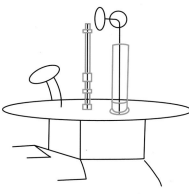

① Start with a stick figure frame of the rover. Use ovals to draw the solar panel and lines to draw the antennae and cameras.

② Now, add detail to the antenna on the line from the previous step, as shown.

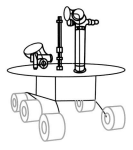

3 Next, draw the cameras and the other antenna.

4 Now, draw the wheels of the vehicle, as shown.

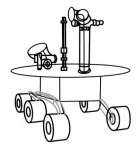

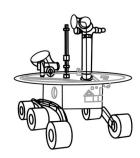

5 In this step, draw curved lines near the wheels, as shown.

6 Draw the details on the solar panel and other parts.

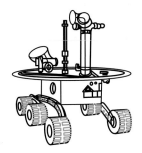

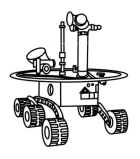

7 Now, draw small rectangles on the surface of the wheels.

8 Erase the extra lines and the stick figure.

9 Color the picture.

What Are SATELLITES?

Satellites in **orbit** around Earth add to human knowledge of the planet. With satellites, scientists can study Earth from a distance and view large areas. Pictures from space provide information that helps explain why Earth looks the way it does and where changes are taking place. By studying Earth from both space and the ground, scientists can learn more about the ever-changing planet.

1957
The year Sputnik I, the first satellite, was launched into space.

2,000
The approximate number of active satellites orbiting Earth.

Frame
A satellite's frame is usually made of a lightweight metal. The frame houses much of the technology that keeps the satellite operating.

 YOU CAN DRAW

Onboard Computer
An onboard computer monitors the satellite's operating system. This system controls the satellite and tells it what to do.

Solar Panels
Solar panels provide most of the power needed to operate the satellite. They collect the Sun's energy and use it to power the satellite. Batteries on the frame make sure the satellite works when there is no sunlight.

Motor
Rocket motors move the satellite to a desired location. Many forces in space cause satellites to drift out of place. Forces that affect a satellite's positioning include solar wind and **gravity**. The motor system powers **thrusters** that can correct a satellite's positioning.

Antennae
Every satellite has a radio system with antennae. This system sends information to and from Earth.

How to Draw a
SATELLITE

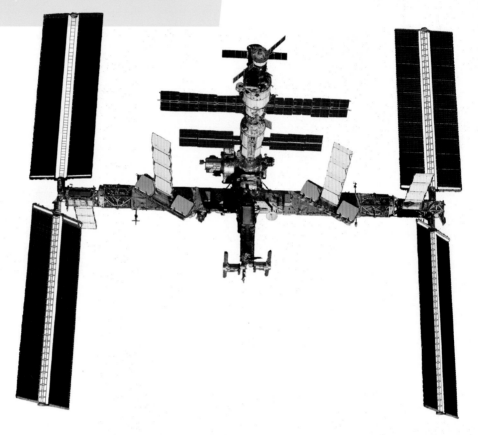

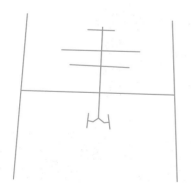

(1) Start with a stick figure frame of the satellite. Use lines to draw the panels and the body.

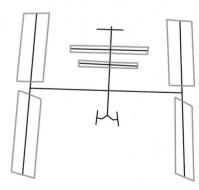

(2) Draw the solar panels by drawing rectangles, as shown.

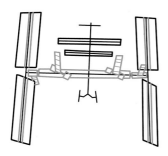

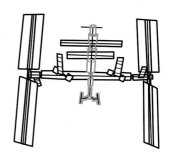

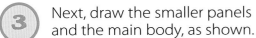

3 Next, draw the smaller panels and the main body, as shown.

4 Now, draw the antenna and cameras using cylinders and rectangles.

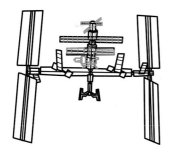

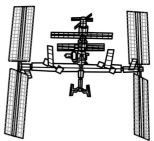

5 In this step, add details to the satellite, as shown.

6 Draw small lines on the solar panels.

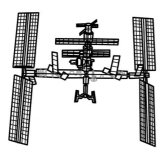

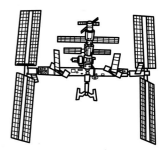

7 Next, draw small lines and circles on other parts of the satellite.

8 Erase the extra lines and the stick figure.

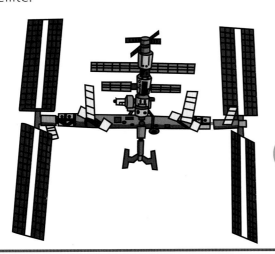

9 Color the picture.

What Is the
SOLAR SYSTEM?

Earth is one of eight planets in our solar system. All of the planets travel around the Sun. Earth, Mars, Mercury, and Venus are called **terrestrial** planets. They consist mainly of rock. Jupiter, Neptune, Saturn, and Uranus are made up mostly of gas. They are called gas giants.

Sun
The Sun is the center of the solar system. The power of the Sun's gravity holds our solar system together. The Sun provides Earth with light, warmth, and a power source.

Mercury
The closest planet to the Sun, Mercury is only slightly larger than Earth's Moon. Mercury is named after the Roman messenger god.

Venus
Venus is the brightest planet and can sometimes be seen with the naked eye. Venus is named after the Roman goddess of love and beauty.

Mars
The second-closest planet to Earth, Mars is home to the largest volcano in our solar system. Mars is named after the Roman god of war.

Neptune
Neptune has the strongest and fastest winds in Earth's solar system. They can reach speeds of 1,500 miles (2,414 km) per hour. Neptune is named after the Roman god of the sea.

Jupiter
Jupiter is the largest planet in our solar system. It is so big that all the other planets in our solar system could fit inside of it. Jupiter is named after the Roman king of the gods.

Saturn
Saturn is known for its colorful rings. Even though it is the second biggest planet, it is the lightest. Saturn is named after the Roman god of farming.

Uranus
Unlike the other planets in our solar system, Uranus' **axis** points toward the Sun. It is named after the Roman god of the sky.

Earth
The **densest** planet in our solar system, Earth has more water on its surface than land. "Earth" means ground or soil.

How to Draw the
SOLAR SYSTEM

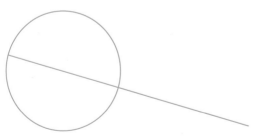

(1) Start with a stick figure frame of the solar system. Draw a circle for the Sun, and a line across it.

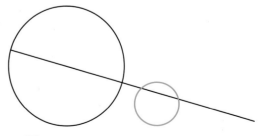

(2) Now, draw Jupiter on the line from the previous step.

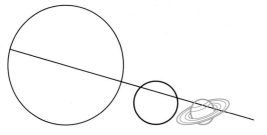

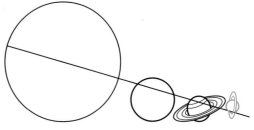

3 Draw Saturn and the ring around it, as shown.

4 Now, using a circle, draw Uranus and the ring around it.

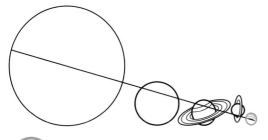

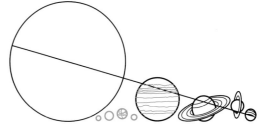

5 In this step, draw Neptune.

6 Next, add details to Jupiter, and draw Mercury, Venus, Earth, and Mars in order from the Sun.

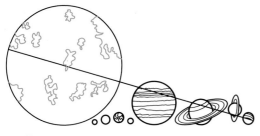

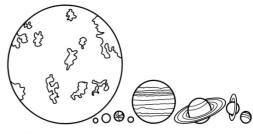

7 Now, draw small curvy figures on the surface of the Sun.

8 Erase the extra lines and the stick figure.

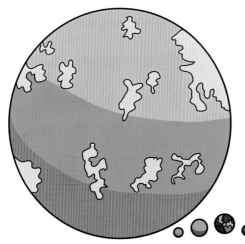

9 Color the picture.

What Is a
SPACE SHUTTLE?

The space shuttle was a type of spaceship built by NASA in the 1980s. It was used to carry people and cargo from Earth to space. Sometimes, the shuttle linked up with the International Space Station. Other times, the shuttle was sent to space to repair a satellite. The shuttle was known for its ability to fly into space like a rocket, orbit around Earth like a satellite, and land like an airplane.

Orbiter
The orbiter was the place where the crew lived and worked. It had a big bay for carrying cargo into space. The orbiter had three main engines for reaching orbit and wings for returning safely back down through the **atmosphere**.

Payload Doors
The payload doors opened to reveal the cargo bay. This was where equipment and machinery, such as satellites, were kept until they were put into space.

2011
The year the last space shuttle mission took place.

178,000
The weight, in pounds, of *Columbia*, the heaviest space shuttle. (80,700 kilograms)

External Tank

The external tank carried 528,000 gallons (2.1 million liters) of liquid hydrogen and liquid oxygen as fuel for the engines in the orbiter.

Rocket Booster

The rocket boosters helped push the orbiter and the external tank along for the first two minutes of flight. The boosters weighed about 650 tons (590 tonnes).

Main Engines

The shuttle had three main engines that were used once the rocket boosters fell off. They could move the shuttle at speeds of up to 17,000 miles (27,358 km) per hour.

How to Draw a
SPACE SHUTTLE

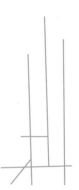

1 Start with a stick figure frame of the space shuttle. Use straight lines to draw the frame.

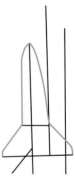

2 Draw the orbiter, as shown.

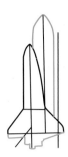
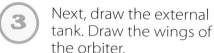
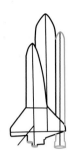

3 Next, draw the external tank. Draw the wings of the orbiter.

4 Now, draw one of the rocket boosters and the thrusters for the orbiter.

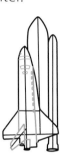
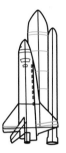

5 In this step, draw the rudder, doors, hatches, and engines of the orbiter.

6 Draw lines on the external tank and wings of the orbiter.

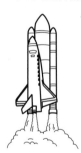

7 Next, draw the other rocket booster, and draw lines on the surface of both the boosters. Draw the smoke clouds, as shown.

8 Erase the extra lines and the stick figure.

9 Color the picture.

Quiz Yourself on
SPACE

01 What material is used to coat the front bubble of an astronaut's helmet to filter out the Sun's rays?

02 Why are spacesuits white?

03 What are three things a Moon base would need?

04 What was the name of the first rover to land on Mars?

05 Approximately how many satellites currently orbit Earth?

06 What are two forces that can cause a satellite to drift out of place?

07 How many planets are in our solar system?

08 Which is the largest planet in our solar system?

09 How much did a space shuttle's rocket boosters weigh?

10 In what year did the last space shuttle mission take place?

ANSWER
01 Gold **02** White reflects heat, **03** Housing, laboratories, and lunar vehicles **04** Sojourner **05** 2,000 **06** Solar wind and gravity **07** Eight **08** Jupiter **09** About 650 tons (590 t) **10** 2011

KEY WORDS

atmosphere: the layer of gases that surrounds Earth

axis: an imaginary line on which a planet spins

cleats: small spikes that dig into the ground

communicate: to send and receive information

densest: the most closely packed together

gravity: a force that moves things toward the center of a planet

life support: a system that keeps astronauts alive

NASA: National Aeronautics and Space Administration

orbit: to move in a path around a planet or other space object

radio system: a communication system that sends and receives information through electromagnetic waves

space debris: small objects that float in space

terrestrial: from Earth or on Earth

thrusters: systems that create force to move the shuttle

INDEX

Get the best of both worlds.

AV2 bridges the gap between print and digital.

The expandable resources toolbar enables quick access to content including **videos**, **audio**, **activities**, **weblinks**, **slideshows**, **quizzes**, and **key words**.

Animated videos make static images come alive.

Resource icons on each page help readers to further **explore key concepts**.

Published by AV2
350 5th Avenue, 59th Floor
New York, NY 10118
Website: www.av2books.com

Library of Congress Cataloging-in-Publication Data
Names: McGill, Jordan, author.
Title: Space / Jordan McGill.
Description: New York, NY : AV2, [2021] | Series: You can draw | Includes index. | Audience: Ages 10-12 | Audience: Grades 4-6 |
Identifiers: LCCN 2019050522 (print) | LCCN 2019050523 (ebook) | ISBN 9781791119751 (library binding) |
    ISBN 9781791119768 (paperback) | ISBN 9781791119775 | ISBN 9781791119782
Subjects: LCSH: Outer space--In art--Juvenile literature. | Astronautics in art--Juvenile literature. | Drawing--Technique--
    Juvenile literature.
Classification: LCC NC825.O9 M39 2021 (print) | LCC NC825.O9 (ebook) |
    DDC 704.9/496294--dc23
LC record available at https://lccn.loc.gov/2019050522
LC ebook record available at https://lccn.loc.gov/2019050523

Printed in Guangzhou, China
1 2 3 4 5 6 7 8 9 0 24 23 22 21 20

042020
101319

Project Coordinator: Heather Kissock
Designer: Terry Paulhus